Getting Shit Done Is The Best Way To Predict The Future

This Notebook Belongs To:

_____

E-mail:

Phone:

2017

January

Su	M	Tu	W	Th	F	Sa
1	2	3	4	5	6	7
8	9	10	11	12	13	14
15	16	17	18	19	20	21
22	23	24	25	26	27	28
29	30	31				

February

Su	M	Tu	W	Th	F	Sa
			1	2	3	4
5	6	7	8	9	10	11
12	13	14	15	16	17	18
19	20	21	22	23	24	25
26	27	28				

March

Su	M	Tu	W	Th	F	Sa
			1	2	3	4
5	6	7	8	9	10	11
12	13	14	15	16	17	18
19	20	21	22	23	24	25
26	27	28	29	30	31	

April

Su	M	Tu	W	Th	F	Sa
						1
2	3	4	5	6	7	8
9	10	11	12	13	14	15
16	17	18	19	20	21	22
23	24	25	26	27	28	29
30						

May

Su	M	Tu	W	Th	F	Sa
	1	2	3	4	5	6
7	8	9	10	11	12	13
14	15	16	17	18	19	20
21	22	23	24	25	26	27
28	29	30	31			

June

Su	M	Tu	W	Th	F	Sa
				1	2	3
4	5	6	7	8	9	10
11	12	13	14	15	16	17
18	19	20	21	22	23	24
25	26	27	28	29	30	

July

Su	M	Tu	W	Th	F	Sa
						1
2	3	4	5	6	7	8
9	10	11	12	13	14	15
16	17	18	19	20	21	22
23	24	25	26	27	28	29
30	31					

August

Su	M	Tu	W	Th	F	Sa
		1	2	3	4	5
6	7	8	9	10	11	12
13	14	15	16	17	18	19
20	21	22	23	24	25	26
27	28	29	30	31		

September

Su	M	Tu	W	Th	F	Sa
					1	2
3	4	5	6	7	8	9
10	11	12	13	14	15	16
17	18	19	20	21	22	23
24	25	26	27	28	29	30

October

Su	M	Tu	W	Th	F	Sa
1	2	3	4	5	6	7
8	9	10	11	12	13	14
15	16	17	18	19	20	21
22	23	24	25	26	27	28
29	30	31				

November

Su	M	Tu	W	Th	F	Sa
			1	2	3	4
5	6	7	8	9	10	11
12	13	14	15	16	17	18
19	20	21	22	23	24	25
26	27	28	29	30		

December

Su	M	Tu	W	Th	F	Sa
					1	2
3	4	5	6	7	8	9
10	11	12	13	14	15	16
17	18	19	20	21	22	23
24	25	26	27	28	29	30
31						

Date   Special Occasions

DATE:

Schedule:

7:00

8:00

9:00

10:00

11:00

12:00

1:00

2:00

3:00

4:00

5:00

To Do List:

❑

❑

❑

❑

❑

❑

❑

❑

Time for Me:
❑ Rejuvenation Break 1
❑ Lunch
❑ Rejuvenation Break 2
❑ Exercise
❑ Other: _____

Notes, Ideas, & Thoughts :

DATE:

Schedule:

7:00

8:00

9:00

10:00

11:00

12:00

1:00

2:00

3:00

4:00

5:00

To Do List:

❑

❑

❑

❑

❑

❑

❑

❑

Time for Me:
❑ Rejuvenation Break 1
❑ Lunch
❑ Rejuvenation Break 2
❑ Exercise
❑ Other: _____

Notes, Ideas, & Thoughts :

Schedule:

7:00

8:00

9:00

10:00

11:00

12:00

1:00

2:00

3:00

4:00

5:00

To Do List:

❑

❑

❑

❑

❑

❑

❑

Time for Me:
❑ Rejuvenation Break 1
❑ Lunch
❑ Rejuvenation Break 2
❑ Exercise
❑ Other: _____

Notes, Ideas, & Thoughts :

Schedule:

7:00

8:00

9:00

10:00

11:00

12:00

1:00

2:00

3:00

4:00

5:00

To Do List:

❑

❑

❑

❑

❑

❑

❑

❑

Time for Me:
❑ Rejuvenation Break 1
❑ Lunch
❑ Rejuvenation Break 2
❑ Exercise
❑ Other: _____

Notes, Ideas, & Thoughts :

Schedule:

7:00

8:00

9:00

10:00

11:00

12:00

1:00

2:00

3:00

4:00

5:00

To Do List:

❑

❑

❑

❑

❑

❑

❑

❑

Time for Me:
❑ Rejuvenation Break 1
❑ Lunch
❑ Rejuvenation Break 2
❑ Exercise
❑ Other: _____

Notes, Ideas, & Thoughts :

Schedule:

7:00

8:00

9:00

10:00

11:00

12:00

1:00

2:00

3:00

4:00

5:00

To Do List:

❑

❑

❑

❑

❑

❑

❑

❑

Time for Me:
❑ Rejuvenation Break 1
❑ Lunch
❑ Rejuvenation Break 2
❑ Exercise
❑ Other: _____

Notes, Ideas, & Thoughts :

Schedule:

7:00

8:00

9:00

10:00

11:00

12:00

1:00

2:00

3:00

4:00

5:00

To Do List:

❑

❑

❑

❑

❑

❑

❑

❑

Time for Me:
❑ Rejuvenation Break 1
❑ Lunch
❑ Rejuvenation Break 2
❑ Exercise
❑ Other: _____

Notes, Ideas, & Thoughts :

DATE:

Schedule:

7:00

8:00

9:00

10:00

11:00

12:00

1:00

2:00

3:00

4:00

5:00

To Do List:

❑

❑

❑

❑

❑

❑

❑

❑

Time for Me:
❑ Rejuvenation Break 1
❑ Lunch
❑ Rejuvenation Break 2
❑ Exercise
❑ Other: _____

Notes, Ideas, & Thoughts :

Schedule:

7:00

8:00

9:00

10:00

11:00

12:00

1:00

2:00

3:00

4:00

5:00

To Do List:

❑

❑

❑

❑

❑

❑

❑

❑

Time for Me:
❑ Rejuvenation Break 1
❑ Lunch
❑ Rejuvenation Break 2
❑ Exercise
❑ Other: _____

Notes, Ideas, & Thoughts :

DATE:

Schedule:

7:00

8:00

9:00

10:00

11:00

12:00

1:00

2:00

3:00

4:00

5:00

To Do List:

☐

☐

☐

☐

☐

☐

☐

☐

Time for Me:
☐ Rejuvenation Break 1
☐ Lunch
☐ Rejuvenation Break 2
☐ Exercise
☐ Other: _____

Notes, Ideas, & Thoughts :

Schedule:

7:00

8:00

9:00

10:00

11:00

12:00

1:00

2:00

3:00

4:00

5:00

To Do List:

❑

❑

❑

❑

❑

❑

❑

❑

Time for Me:
❑ Rejuvenation Break 1
❑ Lunch
❑ Rejuvenation Break 2
❑ Exercise
❑ Other: _____

Notes, Ideas, & Thoughts :

Schedule:

7:00

8:00

9:00

10:00

11:00

12:00

1:00

2:00

3:00

4:00

5:00

To Do List:

❑

❑

❑

❑

❑

❑

❑

❑

Time for Me:
❑ Rejuvenation Break 1
❑ Lunch
❑ Rejuvenation Break 2
❑ Exercise
❑ Other: _____

Notes, Ideas, & Thoughts :

Schedule:

7:00

8:00

9:00

10:00

11:00

12:00

1:00

2:00

3:00

4:00

5:00

To Do List:

❑

❑

❑

❑

❑

❑

❑

❑

Time for Me:
❑ Rejuvenation Break 1
❑ Lunch
❑ Rejuvenation Break 2
❑ Exercise
❑ Other: _____

Notes, Ideas, & Thoughts :

DATE:

Schedule:

7:00

8:00

9:00

10:00

11:00

12:00

1:00

2:00

3:00

4:00

5:00

To Do List:

☐

☐

☐

☐

☐

☐

☐

☐

Time for Me:
☐ Rejuvenation Break 1
☐ Lunch
☐ Rejuvenation Break 2
☐ Exercise
☐ Other: _____

Notes, Ideas, & Thoughts :

Schedule:

7:00

8:00

9:00

10:00

11:00

12:00

1:00

2:00

3:00

4:00

5:00

To Do List:

❑

❑

❑

❑

❑

❑

❑

❑

Time for Me:
❑ Rejuvenation Break 1
❑ Lunch
❑ Rejuvenation Break 2
❑ Exercise
❑ Other: _____

Notes, Ideas, & Thoughts :

DATE:

Schedule:

7:00

8:00

9:00

10:00

11:00

12:00

1:00

2:00

3:00

4:00

5:00

To Do List:

❑

❑

❑

❑

❑

❑

❑

❑

Time for Me:
❑ Rejuvenation Break 1
❑ Lunch
❑ Rejuvenation Break 2
❑ Exercise
❑ Other: _____

Notes, Ideas, & Thoughts :

Schedule:

7:00

8:00

9:00

10:00

11:00

12:00

1:00

2:00

3:00

4:00

5:00

To Do List:

☐

☐

☐

☐

☐

☐

☐

☐

Time for Me:
☐ Rejuvenation Break 1
☐ Lunch
☐ Rejuvenation Break 2
☐ Exercise
☐ Other: _____

Notes, Ideas, & Thoughts :

DATE:

Schedule:

7:00

8:00

9:00

10:00

11:00

12:00

1:00

2:00

3:00

4:00

5:00

To Do List:

☐

☐

☐

☐

☐

☐

☐

☐

Time for Me:
☐ Rejuvenation Break 1
☐ Lunch
☐ Rejuvenation Break 2
☐ Exercise
☐ Other: _____

Notes, Ideas, & Thoughts :

Schedule:

7:00

8:00

9:00

10:00

11:00

12:00

1:00

2:00

3:00

4:00

5:00

To Do List:

❑

❑

❑

❑

❑

❑

❑

❑

Time for Me:
❑ Rejuvenation Break 1
❑ Lunch
❑ Rejuvenation Break 2
❑ Exercise
❑ Other: _____

Notes, Ideas, & Thoughts :

Schedule:

7:00

8:00

9:00

10:00

11:00

12:00

1:00

2:00

3:00

4:00

5:00

To Do List:

☐

☐

☐

☐

☐

☐

☐

☐

Time for Me:
☐ Rejuvenation Break 1
☐ Lunch
☐ Rejuvenation Break 2
☐ Exercise
☐ Other: _____

Notes, Ideas, & Thoughts :

Schedule:

7:00

8:00

9:00

10:00

11:00

12:00

1:00

2:00

3:00

4:00

5:00

To Do List:

❑

❑

❑

❑

❑

❑

❑

❑

Time for Me:
❑ Rejuvenation Break 1
❑ Lunch
❑ Rejuvenation Break 2
❑ Exercise
❑ Other: _____

Notes, Ideas, & Thoughts :

Schedule:

7:00

8:00

9:00

10:00

11:00

12:00

1:00

2:00

3:00

4:00

5:00

To Do List:

☐

☐

☐

☐

☐

☐

☐

☐

Time for Me:
☐ Rejuvenation Break 1
☐ Lunch
☐ Rejuvenation Break 2
☐ Exercise
☐ Other: _____

Notes, Ideas, & Thoughts :

DATE:

Schedule:

7:00

8:00

9:00

10:00

11:00

12:00

1:00

2:00

3:00

4:00

5:00

To Do List:

❑

❑

❑

❑

❑

❑

❑

❑

Time for Me:
❑ Rejuvenation Break 1
❑ Lunch
❑ Rejuvenation Break 2
❑ Exercise
❑ Other: _____

Notes, Ideas, & Thoughts :

DATE:

Schedule:

7:00	
8:00	
9:00	
10:00	
11:00	
12:00	
1:00	
2:00	
3:00	
4:00	
5:00	

To Do List:

- ☐
- ☐
- ☐
- ☐
- ☐
- ☐
- ☐
- ☐

Time for Me:
- ☐ Rejuvenation Break 1
- ☐ Lunch
- ☐ Rejuvenation Break 2
- ☐ Exercise
- ☐ Other: _____

Notes, Ideas, & Thoughts :

DATE:

Schedule:

7:00

8:00

9:00

10:00

11:00

12:00

1:00

2:00

3:00

4:00

5:00

To Do List:

☐

☐

☐

☐

☐

☐

☐

☐

Time for Me:
☐ Rejuvenation Break 1
☐ Lunch
☐ Rejuvenation Break 2
☐ Exercise
☐ Other: _____

Notes, Ideas, & Thoughts :

DATE:

Schedule:

7:00

8:00

9:00

10:00

11:00

12:00

1:00

2:00

3:00

4:00

5:00

To Do List:

❑

❑

❑

❑

❑

❑

❑

❑

Time for Me:
❑ Rejuvenation Break 1
❑ Lunch
❑ Rejuvenation Break 2
❑ Exercise
❑ Other: _____

Notes, Ideas, & Thoughts :

Schedule:

7:00

8:00

9:00

10:00

11:00

12:00

1:00

2:00

3:00

4:00

5:00

To Do List:

❑

❑

❑

❑

❑

❑

❑

❑

Time for Me:
❑ Rejuvenation Break 1
❑ Lunch
❑ Rejuvenation Break 2
❑ Exercise
❑ Other: _____

Notes, Ideas, & Thoughts :

Schedule:

7:00

8:00

9:00

10:00

11:00

12:00

1:00

2:00

3:00

4:00

5:00

To Do List:

☐

☐

☐

☐

☐

☐

☐

☐

Time for Me:
☐ Rejuvenation Break 1
☐ Lunch
☐ Rejuvenation Break 2
☐ Exercise
☐ Other: _____

Notes, Ideas, & Thoughts :

Schedule:

7:00

8:00

9:00

10:00

11:00

12:00

1:00

2:00

3:00

4:00

5:00

To Do List:

❑

❑

❑

❑

❑

❑

❑

❑

Time for Me:
❑ Rejuvenation Break 1
❑ Lunch
❑ Rejuvenation Break 2
❑ Exercise
❑ Other: _____

Notes, Ideas, & Thoughts :

DATE:

Schedule:

7:00

8:00

9:00

10:00

11:00

12:00

1:00

2:00

3:00

4:00

5:00

To Do List:

❑

❑

❑

❑

❑

❑

❑

❑

Time for Me:
❑ Rejuvenation Break 1
❑ Lunch
❑ Rejuvenation Break 2
❑ Exercise
❑ Other: _____

Notes, Ideas, & Thoughts :

Schedule:

7:00

8:00

9:00

10:00

11:00

12:00

1:00

2:00

3:00

4:00

5:00

To Do List:

❑

❑

❑

❑

❑

❑

❑

❑

Time for Me:
❑ Rejuvenation Break 1
❑ Lunch
❑ Rejuvenation Break 2
❑ Exercise
❑ Other: _____

Notes, Ideas, & Thoughts :

DATE:

Schedule:

7:00

8:00

9:00

10:00

11:00

12:00

1:00

2:00

3:00

4:00

5:00

To Do List:

☐

☐

☐

☐

☐

☐

☐

☐

Time for Me:
☐ Rejuvenation Break 1
☐ Lunch
☐ Rejuvenation Break 2
☐ Exercise
☐ Other: _____

Notes, Ideas, & Thoughts :

DATE:

Schedule:

7:00

8:00

9:00

10:00

11:00

12:00

1:00

2:00

3:00

4:00

5:00

To Do List:

❑

❑

❑

❑

❑

❑

❑

❑

Time for Me:
❑ Rejuvenation Break 1
❑ Lunch
❑ Rejuvenation Break 2
❑ Exercise
❑ Other: _____

Notes, Ideas, & Thoughts :

Schedule:

7:00

8:00

9:00

10:00

11:00

12:00

1:00

2:00

3:00

4:00

5:00

To Do List:

☐

☐

☐

☐

☐

☐

☐

☐

Time for Me:
☐ Rejuvenation Break 1
☐ Lunch
☐ Rejuvenation Break 2
☐ Exercise
☐ Other: _____

Notes, Ideas, & Thoughts :

Schedule:

7:00

8:00

9:00

10:00

11:00

12:00

1:00

2:00

3:00

4:00

5:00

To Do List:

❑

❑

❑

❑

❑

❑

❑

❑

Time for Me:
❑ Rejuvenation Break 1
❑ Lunch
❑ Rejuvenation Break 2
❑ Exercise
❑ Other: _____

Notes, Ideas, & Thoughts :

Schedule:

7:00

8:00

9:00

10:00

11:00

12:00

1:00

2:00

3:00

4:00

5:00

To Do List:

- ☐
- ☐
- ☐
- ☐
- ☐
- ☐
- ☐
- ☐

Time for Me:
- ☐ Rejuvenation Break 1
- ☐ Lunch
- ☐ Rejuvenation Break 2
- ☐ Exercise
- ☐ Other: _____

Notes, Ideas, & Thoughts :

Schedule:

7:00

8:00

9:00

10:00

11:00

12:00

1:00

2:00

3:00

4:00

5:00

To Do List:

❑

❑

❑

❑

❑

❑

❑

❑

Time for Me:
❑ Rejuvenation Break 1
❑ Lunch
❑ Rejuvenation Break 2
❑ Exercise
❑ Other: _____

Notes, Ideas, & Thoughts :

Schedule:

7:00

8:00

9:00

10:00

11:00

12:00

1:00

2:00

3:00

4:00

5:00

To Do List:

❑

❑

❑

❑

❑

❑

❑

❑

Time for Me:
❑ Rejuvenation Break 1
❑ Lunch
❑ Rejuvenation Break 2
❑ Exercise
❑ Other: _____

Notes, Ideas, & Thoughts :

Schedule:

7:00

8:00

9:00

10:00

11:00

12:00

1:00

2:00

3:00

4:00

5:00

To Do List:

❑

❑

❑

❑

❑

❑

❑

❑

Time for Me:
❑ Rejuvenation Break 1
❑ Lunch
❑ Rejuvenation Break 2
❑ Exercise
❑ Other: _____

Notes, Ideas, & Thoughts :

Schedule:

7:00

8:00

9:00

10:00

11:00

12:00

1:00

2:00

3:00

4:00

5:00

To Do List:

☐

☐

☐

☐

☐

☐

☐

☐

Time for Me:
☐ Rejuvenation Break 1
☐ Lunch
☐ Rejuvenation Break 2
☐ Exercise
☐ Other: _____

Notes, Ideas, & Thoughts :

Schedule:

7:00

8:00

9:00

10:00

11:00

12:00

1:00

2:00

3:00

4:00

5:00

To Do List:

❑

❑

❑

❑

❑

❑

❑

Time for Me:
❑ Rejuvenation Break 1
❑ Lunch
❑ Rejuvenation Break 2
❑ Exercise
❑ Other: _____

Notes, Ideas, & Thoughts :

Schedule:

7:00

8:00

9:00

10:00

11:00

12:00

1:00

2:00

3:00

4:00

5:00

To Do List:

☐

☐

☐

☐

☐

☐

☐

☐

Time for Me:
☐ Rejuvenation Break 1
☐ Lunch
☐ Rejuvenation Break 2
☐ Exercise
☐ Other: _____

Notes, Ideas, & Thoughts :

Schedule:

7:00

8:00

9:00

10:00

11:00

12:00

1:00

2:00

3:00

4:00

5:00

To Do List:

❑

❑

❑

❑

❑

❑

❑

❑

Time for Me:
❑ Rejuvenation Break 1
❑ Lunch
❑ Rejuvenation Break 2
❑ Exercise
❑ Other: _____

Notes, Ideas, & Thoughts :

DATE:

Schedule:

7:00

8:00

9:00

10:00

11:00

12:00

1:00

2:00

3:00

4:00

5:00

To Do List:

☐

☐

☐

☐

☐

☐

☐

☐

Time for Me:
☐ Rejuvenation Break 1
☐ Lunch
☐ Rejuvenation Break 2
☐ Exercise
☐ Other: _____

Notes, Ideas, & Thoughts :

Schedule:

7:00

8:00

9:00

10:00

11:00

12:00

1:00

2:00

3:00

4:00

5:00

To Do List:

❑

❑

❑

❑

❑

❑

❑

❑

Time for Me:
❑ Rejuvenation Break 1
❑ Lunch
❑ Rejuvenation Break 2
❑ Exercise
❑ Other: _____

Notes, Ideas, & Thoughts :

Schedule:

7:00

8:00

9:00

10:00

11:00

12:00

1:00

2:00

3:00

4:00

5:00

To Do List:

❑

❑

❑

❑

❑

❑

❑

❑

Time for Me:
❑ Rejuvenation Break 1
❑ Lunch
❑ Rejuvenation Break 2
❑ Exercise
❑ Other: _____

Notes, Ideas, & Thoughts :

DATE:

Schedule:

7:00

8:00

9:00

10:00

11:00

12:00

1:00

2:00

3:00

4:00

5:00

To Do List:

❑

❑

❑

❑

❑

❑

❑

❑

Time for Me:
❑ Rejuvenation Break 1
❑ Lunch
❑ Rejuvenation Break 2
❑ Exercise
❑ Other: _____

Notes, Ideas, & Thoughts :

Schedule:

7:00

8:00

9:00

10:00

11:00

12:00

1:00

2:00

3:00

4:00

5:00

To Do List:

❑

❑

❑

❑

❑

❑

❑

❑

Time for Me:
❑ Rejuvenation Break 1
❑ Lunch
❑ Rejuvenation Break 2
❑ Exercise
❑ Other: _____

Notes, Ideas, & Thoughts :

Schedule:

7:00

8:00

9:00

10:00

11:00

12:00

1:00

2:00

3:00

4:00

5:00

To Do List:

❏

❏

❏

❏

❏

❏

❏

❏

Time for Me:
❏ Rejuvenation Break 1
❏ Lunch
❏ Rejuvenation Break 2
❏ Exercise
❏ Other: _____

Notes, Ideas, & Thoughts :

DATE:

Schedule:

7:00

8:00

9:00

10:00

11:00

12:00

1:00

2:00

3:00

4:00

5:00

To Do List:

☐

☐

☐

☐

☐

☐

☐

☐

Time for Me:
☐ Rejuvenation Break 1
☐ Lunch
☐ Rejuvenation Break 2
☐ Exercise
☐ Other: _____

Notes, Ideas, & Thoughts :

Schedule:

7:00

8:00

9:00

10:00

11:00

12:00

1:00

2:00

3:00

4:00

5:00

To Do List:

❑

❑

❑

❑

❑

❑

❑

❑

Time for Me:
❑ Rejuvenation Break 1
❑ Lunch
❑ Rejuvenation Break 2
❑ Exercise
❑ Other: _____

Notes, Ideas, & Thoughts :

Schedule:

7:00

8:00

9:00

10:00

11:00

12:00

1:00

2:00

3:00

4:00

5:00

To Do List:

❑

❑

❑

❑

❑

❑

❑

❑

Time for Me:
❑ Rejuvenation Break 1
❑ Lunch
❑ Rejuvenation Break 2
❑ Exercise
❑ Other: _____

Notes, Ideas, & Thoughts :

DATE:

Schedule:

7:00

8:00

9:00

10:00

11:00

12:00

1:00

2:00

3:00

4:00

5:00

To Do List:

❑

❑

❑

❑

❑

❑

❑

❑

Time for Me:
❑ Rejuvenation Break 1
❑ Lunch
❑ Rejuvenation Break 2
❑ Exercise
❑ Other: _____

Notes, Ideas, & Thoughts :

Schedule:

7:00

8:00

9:00

10:00

11:00

12:00

1:00

2:00

3:00

4:00

5:00

To Do List:

☐

☐

☐

☐

☐

☐

☐

☐

Time for Me:
☐ Rejuvenation Break 1
☐ Lunch
☐ Rejuvenation Break 2
☐ Exercise
☐ Other: _____

Notes, Ideas, & Thoughts :

DATE:

Schedule:

7:00

8:00

9:00

10:00

11:00

12:00

1:00

2:00

3:00

4:00

5:00

To Do List:

❑

❑

❑

❑

❑

❑

❑

❑

Time for Me:
❑ Rejuvenation Break 1
❑ Lunch
❑ Rejuvenation Break 2
❑ Exercise
❑ Other: _____

Notes, Ideas, & Thoughts :

DATE:

Schedule:

7:00

8:00

9:00

10:00

11:00

12:00

1:00

2:00

3:00

4:00

5:00

To Do List:

❑

❑

❑

❑

❑

❑

❑

❑

Time for Me:
❑ Rejuvenation Break 1
❑ Lunch
❑ Rejuvenation Break 2
❑ Exercise
❑ Other: _____

Notes, Ideas, & Thoughts :

DATE:

Schedule:

7:00

8:00

9:00

10:00

11:00

12:00

1:00

2:00

3:00

4:00

5:00

To Do List:

❑

❑

❑

❑

❑

❑

❑

❑

Time for Me:
❑ Rejuvenation Break 1
❑ Lunch
❑ Rejuvenation Break 2
❑ Exercise
❑ Other: _____

Notes, Ideas, & Thoughts :

DATE:

Schedule:

7:00

8:00

9:00

10:00

11:00

12:00

1:00

2:00

3:00

4:00

5:00

To Do List:

❑

❑

❑

❑

❑

❑

❑

❑

Time for Me:
❑ Rejuvenation Break 1
❑ Lunch
❑ Rejuvenation Break 2
❑ Exercise
❑ Other: _____

Notes, Ideas, & Thoughts :

DATE:

Schedule:

7:00

8:00

9:00

10:00

11:00

12:00

1:00

2:00

3:00

4:00

5:00

To Do List:

❑

❑

❑

❑

❑

❑

❑

❑

Time for Me:
❑ Rejuvenation Break 1
❑ Lunch
❑ Rejuvenation Break 2
❑ Exercise
❑ Other: _____

Notes, Ideas, & Thoughts :

Schedule:

7:00

8:00

9:00

10:00

11:00

12:00

1:00

2:00

3:00

4:00

5:00

To Do List:

❑

❑

❑

❑

❑

❑

❑

❑

Time for Me:
❑ Rejuvenation Break 1
❑ Lunch
❑ Rejuvenation Break 2
❑ Exercise
❑ Other: _____

Notes, Ideas, & Thoughts :

Schedule:

7:00

8:00

9:00

10:00

11:00

12:00

1:00

2:00

3:00

4:00

5:00

To Do List:

❑

❑

❑

❑

❑

❑

❑

❑

Time for Me:
❑ Rejuvenation Break 1
❑ Lunch
❑ Rejuvenation Break 2
❑ Exercise
❑ Other: _____

Notes, Ideas, & Thoughts :

DATE:

Schedule:

7:00

8:00

9:00

10:00

11:00

12:00

1:00

2:00

3:00

4:00

5:00

To Do List:

☐

☐

☐

☐

☐

☐

☐

☐

Time for Me:
☐ Rejuvenation Break 1
☐ Lunch
☐ Rejuvenation Break 2
☐ Exercise
☐ Other: _____

Notes, Ideas, & Thoughts :

DATE:

Schedule:

7:00

8:00

9:00

10:00

11:00

12:00

1:00

2:00

3:00

4:00

5:00

To Do List:

☐

☐

☐

☐

☐

☐

☐

☐

Time for Me:
☐ Rejuvenation Break 1
☐ Lunch
☐ Rejuvenation Break 2
☐ Exercise
☐ Other: _____

Notes, Ideas, & Thoughts :

Schedule:

7:00

8:00

9:00

10:00

11:00

12:00

1:00

2:00

3:00

4:00

5:00

To Do List:

❑

❑

❑

❑

❑

❑

❑

❑

Time for Me:
❑ Rejuvenation Break 1
❑ Lunch
❑ Rejuvenation Break 2
❑ Exercise
❑ Other: _____

Notes, Ideas, & Thoughts :

DATE:

Schedule:

7:00

8:00

9:00

10:00

11:00

12:00

1:00

2:00

3:00

4:00

5:00

To Do List:

❑

❑

❑

❑

❑

❑

❑

❑

Time for Me:
❑ Rejuvenation Break 1
❑ Lunch
❑ Rejuvenation Break 2
❑ Exercise
❑ Other: _____

Notes, Ideas, & Thoughts :

DATE:

Schedule:

7:00

8:00

9:00

10:00

11:00

12:00

1:00

2:00

3:00

4:00

5:00

To Do List:

❑

❑

❑

❑

❑

❑

❑

Time for Me:
❑ Rejuvenation Break 1
❑ Lunch
❑ Rejuvenation Break 2
❑ Exercise
❑ Other: _____

Notes, Ideas, & Thoughts :

Schedule:

7:00

8:00

9:00

10:00

11:00

12:00

1:00

2:00

3:00

4:00

5:00

To Do List:

☐

☐

☐

☐

☐

☐

☐

☐

Time for Me:
☐ Rejuvenation Break 1
☐ Lunch
☐ Rejuvenation Break 2
☐ Exercise
☐ Other: _____

Notes, Ideas, & Thoughts :

DATE:

Schedule:

7:00

8:00

9:00

10:00

11:00

12:00

1:00

2:00

3:00

4:00

5:00

To Do List:

☐

☐

☐

☐

☐

☐

☐

☐

Time for Me:
☐ Rejuvenation Break 1
☐ Lunch
☐ Rejuvenation Break 2
☐ Exercise
☐ Other: _____

Notes, Ideas, & Thoughts :

Schedule:

7:00

8:00

9:00

10:00

11:00

12:00

1:00

2:00

3:00

4:00

5:00

To Do List:

❑

❑

❑

❑

❑

❑

❑

❑

Time for Me:
❑ Rejuvenation Break 1
❑ Lunch
❑ Rejuvenation Break 2
❑ Exercise
❑ Other: _____

Notes, Ideas, & Thoughts :

DATE:

Schedule:

7:00

8:00

9:00

10:00

11:00

12:00

1:00

2:00

3:00

4:00

5:00

To Do List:

❑

❑

❑

❑

❑

❑

❑

❑

Time for Me:
❑ Rejuvenation Break 1
❑ Lunch
❑ Rejuvenation Break 2
❑ Exercise
❑ Other: _____

Notes, Ideas, & Thoughts :

DATE:

Schedule:

7:00

8:00

9:00

10:00

11:00

12:00

1:00

2:00

3:00

4:00

5:00

To Do List:

❑

❑

❑

❑

❑

❑

❑

❑

Time for Me:
❑ Rejuvenation Break 1
❑ Lunch
❑ Rejuvenation Break 2
❑ Exercise
❑ Other: _____

Notes, Ideas, & Thoughts :

DATE:

Schedule:

7:00

8:00

9:00

10:00

11:00

12:00

1:00

2:00

3:00

4:00

5:00

To Do List:

☐

☐

☐

☐

☐

☐

☐

☐

Time for Me:
☐ Rejuvenation Break 1
☐ Lunch
☐ Rejuvenation Break 2
☐ Exercise
☐ Other: _____

Notes, Ideas, & Thoughts :

Schedule:

7:00

8:00

9:00

10:00

11:00

12:00

1:00

2:00

3:00

4:00

5:00

To Do List:

❑

❑

❑

❑

❑

❑

❑

❑

Time for Me:
❑ Rejuvenation Break 1
❑ Lunch
❑ Rejuvenation Break 2
❑ Exercise
❑ Other: _____

Notes, Ideas, & Thoughts :

DATE:

Schedule:

7:00

8:00

9:00

10:00

11:00

12:00

1:00

2:00

3:00

4:00

5:00

To Do List:

❑

❑

❑

❑

❑

❑

❑

❑

Time for Me:
❑ Rejuvenation Break 1
❑ Lunch
❑ Rejuvenation Break 2
❑ Exercise
❑ Other: _____

Notes, Ideas, & Thoughts :

Schedule:

7:00

8:00

9:00

10:00

11:00

12:00

1:00

2:00

3:00

4:00

5:00

To Do List:

☐

☐

☐

☐

☐

☐

☐

☐

Time for Me:
☐ Rejuvenation Break 1
☐ Lunch
☐ Rejuvenation Break 2
☐ Exercise
☐ Other: _____

Notes, Ideas, & Thoughts :

DATE:

Schedule:

7:00	
8:00	
9:00	
10:00	
11:00	
12:00	
1:00	
2:00	
3:00	
4:00	
5:00	

To Do List:

❑

❑

❑

❑

❑

❑

❑

❑

Time for Me:
❑ Rejuvenation Break 1
❑ Lunch
❑ Rejuvenation Break 2
❑ Exercise
❑ Other: _____

Notes, Ideas, & Thoughts :

Schedule:

7:00

8:00

9:00

10:00

11:00

12:00

1:00

2:00

3:00

4:00

5:00

To Do List:

❑

❑

❑

❑

❑

❑

❑

❑

Time for Me:
❑ Rejuvenation Break 1
❑ Lunch
❑ Rejuvenation Break 2
❑ Exercise
❑ Other: _____

Notes, Ideas, & Thoughts :

Schedule:

7:00

8:00

9:00

10:00

11:00

12:00

1:00

2:00

3:00

4:00

5:00

To Do List:

☐

☐

☐

☐

☐

☐

☐

☐

Time for Me:
☐ Rejuvenation Break 1
☐ Lunch
☐ Rejuvenation Break 2
☐ Exercise
☐ Other: _____

Notes, Ideas, & Thoughts :

Schedule:

7:00

8:00

9:00

10:00

11:00

12:00

1:00

2:00

3:00

4:00

5:00

To Do List:

☐

☐

☐

☐

☐

☐

☐

☐

Time for Me:
☐ Rejuvenation Break 1
☐ Lunch
☐ Rejuvenation Break 2
☐ Exercise
☐ Other: _____

Notes, Ideas, & Thoughts :

DATE:

Schedule:

7:00

8:00

9:00

10:00

11:00

12:00

1:00

2:00

3:00

4:00

5:00

To Do List:

☐

☐

☐

☐

☐

☐

☐

☐

Time for Me:
☐ Rejuvenation Break 1
☐ Lunch
☐ Rejuvenation Break 2
☐ Exercise
☐ Other: _____

Notes, Ideas, & Thoughts :

DATE:

Schedule:

7:00

8:00

9:00

10:00

11:00

12:00

1:00

2:00

3:00

4:00

5:00

To Do List:

☐

☐

☐

☐

☐

☐

☐

☐

Time for Me:
☐ Rejuvenation Break 1
☐ Lunch
☐ Rejuvenation Break 2
☐ Exercise
☐ Other: _____

Notes, Ideas, & Thoughts :

Schedule:

7:00
_____

8:00
_____

9:00
_____

10:00
_____

11:00
_____

12:00
_____

1:00
_____

2:00
_____

3:00
_____

4:00
_____

5:00
_____

To Do List:

❑ _____

❑ _____

❑ _____

❑ _____

❑ _____

❑ _____

❑ _____

❑ _____

Time for Me:
❑ Rejuvenation Break 1
❑ Lunch
❑ Rejuvenation Break 2
❑ Exercise
❑ Other: _____

Notes, Ideas, & Thoughts :

_____

_____

_____

_____

_____

Schedule:

7:00

8:00

9:00

10:00

11:00

12:00

1:00

2:00

3:00

4:00

5:00

To Do List:

❑

❑

❑

❑

❑

❑

❑

❑

Time for Me:
❑ Rejuvenation Break 1
❑ Lunch
❑ Rejuvenation Break 2
❑ Exercise
❑ Other: _____

Notes, Ideas, & Thoughts :

Schedule:

7:00

8:00

9:00

10:00

11:00

12:00

1:00

2:00

3:00

4:00

5:00

To Do List:

❑

❑

❑

❑

❑

❑

❑

❑

Time for Me:
❑ Rejuvenation Break 1
❑ Lunch
❑ Rejuvenation Break 2
❑ Exercise
❑ Other: _____

Notes, Ideas, & Thoughts :

Schedule:

7:00

8:00

9:00

10:00

11:00

12:00

1:00

2:00

3:00

4:00

5:00

To Do List:

❑

❑

❑

❑

❑

❑

❑

❑

Time for Me:
❑ Rejuvenation Break 1
❑ Lunch
❑ Rejuvenation Break 2
❑ Exercise
❑ Other: _____

Notes, Ideas, & Thoughts :

DATE:

Schedule:

7:00

8:00

9:00

10:00

11:00

12:00

1:00

2:00

3:00

4:00

5:00

To Do List:

❑

❑

❑

❑

❑

❑

❑

❑

Time for Me:
❑ Rejuvenation Break 1
❑ Lunch
❑ Rejuvenation Break 2
❑ Exercise
❑ Other: _____

Notes, Ideas, & Thoughts :

Schedule:

7:00

8:00

9:00

10:00

11:00

12:00

1:00

2:00

3:00

4:00

5:00

To Do List:

❑

❑

❑

❑

❑

❑

❑

❑

Time for Me:
❑ Rejuvenation Break 1
❑ Lunch
❑ Rejuvenation Break 2
❑ Exercise
❑ Other: _____

Notes, Ideas, & Thoughts :

DATE:

Schedule:

7:00

8:00

9:00

10:00

11:00

12:00

1:00

2:00

3:00

4:00

5:00

To Do List:

☐

☐

☐

☐

☐

☐

☐

☐

Time for Me:
☐ Rejuvenation Break 1
☐ Lunch
☐ Rejuvenation Break 2
☐ Exercise
☐ Other: _____

Notes, Ideas, & Thoughts :

Schedule:

7:00

8:00

9:00

10:00

11:00

12:00

1:00

2:00

3:00

4:00

5:00

To Do List:

❑

❑

❑

❑

❑

❑

❑

❑

Time for Me:
❑ Rejuvenation Break 1
❑ Lunch
❑ Rejuvenation Break 2
❑ Exercise
❑ Other: _____

Notes, Ideas, & Thoughts :

DATE:

Schedule:

7:00

8:00

9:00

10:00

11:00

12:00

1:00

2:00

3:00

4:00

5:00

To Do List:

❑

❑

❑

❑

❑

❑

❑

❑

Time for Me:
❑ Rejuvenation Break 1
❑ Lunch
❑ Rejuvenation Break 2
❑ Exercise
❑ Other: _____

Notes, Ideas, & Thoughts :

DATE:

Schedule:

7:00

8:00

9:00

10:00

11:00

12:00

1:00

2:00

3:00

4:00

5:00

To Do List:

❑

❑

❑

❑

❑

❑

❑

❑

Time for Me:
❑ Rejuvenation Break 1
❑ Lunch
❑ Rejuvenation Break 2
❑ Exercise
❑ Other: _____

Notes, Ideas, & Thoughts :

Schedule:

7:00

8:00

9:00

10:00

11:00

12:00

1:00

2:00

3:00

4:00

5:00

To Do List:

☐

☐

☐

☐

☐

☐

☐

☐

Time for Me:
☐ Rejuvenation Break 1
☐ Lunch
☐ Rejuvenation Break 2
☐ Exercise
☐ Other: _____

Notes, Ideas, & Thoughts :

Schedule:

7:00

8:00

9:00

10:00

11:00

12:00

1:00

2:00

3:00

4:00

5:00

To Do List:

❑

❑

❑

❑

❑

❑

❑

❑

Time for Me:
❑ Rejuvenation Break 1
❑ Lunch
❑ Rejuvenation Break 2
❑ Exercise
❑ Other: _____

Notes, Ideas, & Thoughts :

Schedule:

7:00

8:00

9:00

10:00

11:00

12:00

1:00

2:00

3:00

4:00

5:00

To Do List:

☐

☐

☐

☐

☐

☐

☐

☐

Time for Me:
☐ Rejuvenation Break 1
☐ Lunch
☐ Rejuvenation Break 2
☐ Exercise
☐ Other: _____

Notes, Ideas, & Thoughts :

DATE:

Schedule:

7:00

8:00

9:00

10:00

11:00

12:00

1:00

2:00

3:00

4:00

5:00

To Do List:

☐

☐

☐

☐

☐

☐

☐

☐

Time for Me:
☐ Rejuvenation Break 1
☐ Lunch
☐ Rejuvenation Break 2
☐ Exercise
☐ Other: _____

Notes, Ideas, & Thoughts :

Schedule:

7:00

8:00

9:00

10:00

11:00

12:00

1:00

2:00

3:00

4:00

5:00

To Do List:

❑

❑

❑

❑

❑

❑

❑

❑

Time for Me:
❑ Rejuvenation Break 1
❑ Lunch
❑ Rejuvenation Break 2
❑ Exercise
❑ Other: _____

Notes, Ideas, & Thoughts :

DATE:

Schedule:

7:00

8:00

9:00

10:00

11:00

12:00

1:00

2:00

3:00

4:00

5:00

To Do List:

☐

☐

☐

☐

☐

☐

☐

☐

Time for Me:
☐ Rejuvenation Break 1
☐ Lunch
☐ Rejuvenation Break 2
☐ Exercise
☐ Other: _____

Notes, Ideas, & Thoughts :

DATE:

Schedule:

7:00

8:00

9:00

10:00

11:00

12:00

1:00

2:00

3:00

4:00

5:00

To Do List:

☐

☐

☐

☐

☐

☐

☐

☐

Time for Me:
☐ Rejuvenation Break 1
☐ Lunch
☐ Rejuvenation Break 2
☐ Exercise
☐ Other: _____

Notes, Ideas, & Thoughts :

Schedule:

7:00

8:00

9:00

10:00

11:00

12:00

1:00

2:00

3:00

4:00

5:00

To Do List:

❑

❑

❑

❑

❑

❑

❑

❑

Time for Me:
❑ Rejuvenation Break 1
❑ Lunch
❑ Rejuvenation Break 2
❑ Exercise
❑ Other: _____

Notes, Ideas, & Thoughts :

For other motivational products including shirts, mugs and other product s, visit:

http://www.cafepress.com/getyourshttogether

61478803R00058

Made in the USA
Lexington, KY
11 March 2017